Visited Mom

Today

Conversations Through the Lens of
Alzheimer's & Dementia

John D. Scully

Green Heart Living Press

ISBN Paperback: 978-1-954493-73-5

Cover design: Matt Scully

Published by Green Heart Living Press

This is a work of creative nonfiction. The events are portrayed to the best of the author's memory. While all the stories in this book are true, names and identifying details have been changed to protect the privacy of the people involved.

CONTENTS

DEDICATION

THIS BOOK IS DEDICATED to everyone who takes care of our loved ones living with Alzheimer's and dementia with patience, warmth, and respect. They are a gift to all of us.

Preface

EACH TIME I VISITED my mother's nursing home, I had conversations with the residents. These conversations started simply and organically as I became comfortable talking to people with dementia. There was always someone to talk to. I would never be able to relay every conversation I had over the years. Most of them were pretty ordinary. But a few years ago, I began making a habit of writing down the ones that stood out, the special ones. Without much thought, I shared one conversation with my friends on Facebook. It was a sweet one and I wanted someone else to witness it. I was not expecting the response I received.

People loved reading the post and thanked me for it. Over time I began sharing more conversations, grabbing more attention with each one. I found my friends and followers waiting for another one or asking when they could expect the next conversation. People said that I should publish a collection, that it would be helpful to families whose loved ones had Alzheimer's/dementia. I dismissed the notion for a time and made excuses for why I couldn't put one together. Thanks to my Facebook friends, I (finally) decided to listen to what my life was asking of me and see where it would lead. Where it led is what you are holding in your hands now.

I have always believed that setting a destination is not nearly as important as the journey that takes you there. When I hear of anyone achieving a goal, I will often ask, "How did this happen?" and "What got you here?" To understand what happened and how I got here, you need to know a part of my story, our family's story.

In May of 2008, our mother was diagnosed with what the doctor called, "dementia of the Alzheimer's type." For two and a half years she was able to live at home with the help of my five siblings and me. We also brought in home care aides to help her take medications, fix small meals, do light housework, and keep her company.

In March of 2011, Mom fell and spent time in the hospital. She was only there a few days, but her body weakened during that time. Doctors said she needed rehabilitation before returning home. She was admitted to a nursing home strictly to do rehab. The plan was to get her walking again and take her home with additional in-home services.

Because her thinking was being affected by the disease, she could not understand why she needed to be there. We explained endlessly that she needed physical therapy to get stronger, but each day she refused to do it. At the 45-day mark the nursing home said, for Mom's safety, they could not discharge her without 24-hour care. She had been in a wheelchair since falling and now needed help with every aspect of personal care. Along with our dad, we made the difficult decision to change her status to permanent resident.

Mom would not mingle with the other residents. She wanted nothing to do with "those people." For two years she sat in her room without leaving, even for meals. When we visited, we also stayed in her room. We only knew her roommate and didn't have an opportunity to talk with other residents.

In 2013, the disease progressed to a point where she was less aware of her surroundings and less inhibited. She was invited to join a memory care program they were starting at the nursing home. It would be housed on a specific unit and was strictly for people with all types of dementia. She would be involved in programs, activities, meals, and socializing from late morning through bedtime. Surprisingly, she was willing to do this. We

5

felt good about the fact that she wasn't sitting in her room all day and was being kept busy with staff and other residents around her. It also gave us an opportunity to start interacting with the recreational staff, other residents, and their family members.

We were now visiting Mom in a large activity room full of people with dementia. To be honest, it was off-putting at first. Some people were sweet and content, while others were angry and agitated. It was eye opening and uncomfortable. But we wanted Mom to be there so her days would be full. I looked forward to seeing her, but I was ambivalent about sitting with everyone else.

In the first months of visiting the memory care program, I watched how the staff interacted with the residents. They knew how to respond to the nuances of each personality. They knew how to diffuse a patient stuck on a topic or patiently answer the same questions repeatedly. Without knowing it, I was learning how to communicate and how to reach the residents in their own worlds.

On one particular evening, I was running very late and didn't get there until 7:30. It had been a long day at work, and I rushed to get there, even though I would have preferred to go home. But what happened at the start of that visit had such an effect on my perspective that I went home and wrote about it. This is what I wrote that evening:

Visited Mom today. Was dressed in a suit, tie, and winter overcoat. Running very late due to a client meeting. Walked into the dining room during evening snack — graham crackers and cranberry juice. As I scanned the room I could hear loud talking and laughing coming from a table of five women residents. I walked in the direction of this raucous table making my way towards Mom. As I got closer to the table this was the conversation:

Ringleader of the fun: (leaning into the table to whisper) "Shhhh ... shhh ... quiet girls. Here comes the minister."

Me: "Well ... sounds like everyone is having a good time tonight!"

Resident Ringleader: "Oh yes, Reverend. It's a lovely wedding."

Me: "Well yes, it is! They sure know how to throw a nice party, don't they?"

Resident: "Oh yes ... and we are on our second glass of wine." (giggling and holding up her glass of cranberry juice)

Me: "Good for you. Now ... no one is driving, right?"

Resident: "Oh heavens no, Reverend. We are staying right here at the hotel!"

Me: "Good! Then I say ... have another!"

They roared with laughter and toasted each other.

I had no idea there could be a sense of community ... with fun and laughter in a dementia unit. It helps to know ... and warms my heart.

This experience began changing everything for me. I began to understand that there was still life being lived there. It was not easy to watch our mom live with this disease, and I'd always felt this journey was something horrible we'd all have to get through. But now I wondered if all of it had to be a terrible experience. Could there be some lighter moments on this journey?

Our mom couldn't talk for the last eight years of her life, so it was nice visiting other people while we were sitting with her. It was good company for all of us. Over the last several years, I made some wonderful connections with many of the residents. Each conversation was a pleasure. But it was the funny, sweet, poignant ones I wrote down. These were like little gifts I wanted to keep. These are the ones that make up this book and the ones I'm happy to share with you.

Before you start reading the conversations, I want to point out a few things. First, I have changed the names of the residents to protect their identities. Second, these conversations are published with respect and deep affection for people living with Alzheimer's and dementia. They are not meant to poke fun or laugh at the ones I had these conversations with. I have been able to establish a good rapport and friendships with people I initially wanted to avoid. These conversations have been a bridge to getting to know them. I hope reading these conversations will help others engage their loved ones, encouraging them to talk and express their feelings. I have laughed, I have cried, I've been fascinated by stories from the past. And being engaged allows our loved ones to continue to experience life.

Lastly, this is my personal experience. I understand not everyone will connect, and some people aren't reachable when they are living with Alzheimer's and dementia. I visited my mother's nursing home for 13 years and experienced that myself with some people. This is a difficult disease. There are many sad, upsetting, and frustrating days when you are dealing with a loved one with Alzheimer's/dementia. But I found an occasional light moment, a personal connection with some wisdom or humor, or sharing a poignant moment with someone can make for cherished memories. Having these conversations is what I did to help make this journey easier.

Eve

Visited Mom today. We sat with Eve, an 80-something resident, at lunch. She didn't say much while she was eating. When she'd finished dessert, she sat back to talk. This was our conversation:

Eve: (pointing to Mom) "Will she be staying here for the summer?"

Me: "Yes, she will. And you?"

Eve: "No. I expect to graduate in May and stay with my parents for the summer."

Me: "Well congratulations. What will you do?"

Eve: "Before I look for my first job, I am going to travel."

Me: "Oh — will you travel with your parents?"

Eve: "Oh God no! They're almost 60 — and no fun!"

She then went through a very detailed itinerary of a trip to Canada.

SALVATORE

VISITED MOM TODAY. WE sat with Salvatore, a burly resident in his late 80s. We check in with each other when our paths cross. He used to work in construction. He told me he was relaxing today. He has a big day tomorrow; he's pouring a building foundation and needs to be on site early. He explained in detail how the foundation will be poured. He hoped the weather wouldn't be too hot. After an update on the job, this was how our conversation ended:

Me: "So then ... has your relaxing day been a good one?"

Salvatore: (thinks for a moment) "I don't know. You tell me."

Me: "Well ... I'm not sure. I haven't been here all day."

It only takes a minute before he smiles.

Salvatore: "It feels like it's been a good day right here. (rubbing his chest) I know I'm happy."

That this kind, gentle man knows he is happy ... makes MY day a good one!

MARGE

VISITED MOM TODAY. WE had lunch with a long-time resident, Marge. She says her dead mother comes to her at night. This was how our conversation wrapped up.

Me: "That is so interesting. How often does she come to you?"

Marge: "She only comes when I'm worried about something or if I've got a problem."

Me: "We always want our mothers when we have a problem, don't we?"

Marge: "She just tells me not to worry … or that things are gonna be okay."

Me: "That's wonderful!"

Marge: "It really makes me feel better."

Me: "Does she visit your sister or anyone else in your family?"

Marge: "Nope. Just me."

Me: "Wow ... isn't that interesting. Why do you think she doesn't appear to your sister?"

Marge: "She can't stand her, like the rest of us!"

JACK

VISITED MOM TODAY. WE sat in the dining room with various residents. There was a new male resident, Jack, walking through. He stopped to say hi and I introduced myself. He said he had recently retired from work. This was our conversation:

Me: "Retirement must be great! What did you do for work?"

Jack: "My mother and I were in steel and iron."

Me: "Really? I'm impressed!"

Jack: "Yes ... I would steal and she would iron."

Even with a dementia diagnosis, his personality comes shining through.

SHIRLEY

VISITED MOM TODAY. I met my brother there, too. A resident named Shirley came into the dining room convinced her lipsticks were missing or stolen. A staff member went to her room and came back with several options of lipsticks. Relieved, Shirley applied her choice while standing at our table talking. When she was done, she said, "I need to check how this looks." Thinking she was going to find a mirror I turned back to my brother to continue our conversation. To my surprise, she stood over me and kissed the top of my bald head ... then stood back and said, "It looks perfect!" She pretended to mess up my "hair" and left us all laughing!

Although confused in many ways, she knew this would be funny and executed it with perfection.

Helen

VISITED MOM TODAY. I talked with Helen, a resident who taught mathematics as a college professor. She is intense. She sometimes lectures like she's still in the classroom. I walked into the TV room. Helen was yelling and frustrated with something she was seeing on her non-existent overhead screen. This was the conversation:

Me: "Hey there. What's going on? You seem frustrated about something."

Helen: "I sure am! Look at this code on the screen. How can I teach when this ridiculous code is in the way?" (There is no code and no screen.)

Me: "Oh geez ... that is annoying."

Helen: "How do they expect me to do my job when this crap keeps happening?"

Me: "That sure is frustrating. Why don't I go to the audio-visual department and let them know you are having problems?"

Helen: "I wish you would."

Me: "Can you get through today the way it is? I think it might take a day to get this fixed."

Helen: "I can, if I don't have to put up with it another day. I've had it."

Me: "I promise, you won't."

Helen: "Oh that's good ... thanks very much." (She immediately calmed down.)

Me: "Is there anything else I can get for you?"

Helen: "No. But thank you. I'm counting on you."

She must have been a helluva professor.

George

Visited Mom today. We walked into George on his hands and knees on the floor. He is a quiet resident who keeps to himself. I stopped to see if he was okay. This was our conversation:

Me: "What are you doing on the floor?

George: (agitated and wiping the floor with his hand) "I need to clean up this mess." (There is nothing there.)

Me: "Why don't we get the custodian to do that?"

George: "I am the custodian."

Me: (after a minute to think) "It's 3:30 pm. Isn't your shift over?"

George: (getting up from the floor) "3:30 already?"

Me: "Yes. I'll get the second shift to clean this up."

George: "Are you sure?"

Me: "Yes — good job today."

George: "Thanks ... I need to go home."

He leaves less agitated — and like all of us — relieved it's quitting time.

PHYLLIS

VISITED MOM TODAY. SHE and I sat in the TV room by ourselves. After lunch, Phyllis came to visit. Out of nowhere, this was our conversation:

Phyllis: "Sooooooo ... I think you might be gay."

Me: " ... and hello to you, too!"

Phyllis: "Am I right?"

Me: "You're very perceptive."

Phyllis: "Well my parents had a gay friend and I used to work with a gay guy. So, I can pick you people out."

Me: "You're very talented."

Phyllis: "People ask me why I like gay people and I tell them ... c'mon, we're all the same inside."

Me: "That's a good response."

Phyllis: "I mean, let's face it ... the only real difference between you and me? ... is I like guys."

Hmmmmmmmm ... a swing and a miss.

JEANNE

VISITED MOM TODAY. WE sat with Jeanne, an 80-something resident, at dinner. She was quiet and pleasant, talking about her meal and checking to see how Mom was doing with her meal. While chatting, she paused for a second with a puzzled look on her face. This was our conversation:

Jeanne: "How old is your mom?"

Me: "She just turned 88."

Jeanne: "God bless her ... and she's here at her job, working hard every single day!"

Me: "You're right. But you're also here at work every day, too."

Jeanne: (smiling and rather smug) "Yes — but I'm half her age."

KAY

VISITED MOM TODAY. I was happy to meet my sister there, too. After lunch, we took Mom to a lounge area in the hallway outside her room. We visited with Kay, a resident who told us she says the rosary every day. We were intrigued she remembered the rosary and touched that it was important to her. She seemed to find comfort in saying it. Because we showed interest, she rushed to find her beads to demonstrate. She blessed herself and then recited the first part of the rosary. She said each of the prayers, without missing a word, and knew how many times it was repeated. She then explained how to move through the beads and finish the rosary. Here was how the conversation ended.

Me: "That is so wonderful you say the rosary every day."

Kay: "We say it downstairs every Tuesday."

Me: "Where do you say it the rest of the week?"

Kay: "I just go in my room and say it."

My Sister: "That is so nice. I know saying the rosary can really give you a sense of peace."

Kay: "It also helps waste some time."

I'm sure the nuns would love to hear that.

Grace

Visited Mom today. I entered the Memory Care unit and practically fell over Grace, a resident sitting in her wheelchair in front of the doors. I was startled. She was just intent on asking me a question. This was our conversation:

Grace: "Did you see my son's father out there?"

Me: "No I didn't. Are you expecting him?"

Grace: "Yeah ... he's coming here to hassle me."

Me: "Really? Hassle you about what?"

Grace: (disgusted) "Ohhhh ... he's looking for a warm place to stay and some food."

Me: "Is that too much to ask?"

Grace: "It is when you're a jerk!"

Hope she stood up to him in the past like she was ready to do today!

MARION

VISITED MOM TODAY. WE walked into the dining room. Sitting alone at a table was Marion, a fairly new resident. She was crying. I sat down beside her. This was our conversation.

Me: "Are you okay?"

Marion: "My husband died today." (He actually died several years ago.)

Me: "Oh no. I'm so sorry to hear that."

Marion: "They just told me. I'm heartbroken."

Me: "What can I do for you?"

Marion: "Will you call my daughter and see where she is? We need to make all the plans."

Me: "The lady at the front desk told me she is on her way."

Marion: "Oh good. I need my family now."

Me: "How about if I sit with you for a while and keep you company?"

Marion: "That would help."

Another cruelty of Alzheimer's/dementia. You can live your worst moments over and over again.

Nancy

Visited Mom today. We sat with Nancy, a resident who told us she has ESP (extra-sensory perception). I was intrigued. This was part of our conversation:

Me: "Wow! I have never met anyone with ESP. That's pretty cool!"

Nancy: "It's a gift my grandmother passed down."

Me: "So ... how do you know you have the gift?"

Nancy: "I just know things."

Me: "Really."

Nancy: "Let me ask you a question."

Me: "Sure ... "

Nancy: "Have you ever been in an accident?"

Me: "I have."

Nancy: "Seeee?" (Her hands were open and proud.)

Me: "See what?"

Nancy: "See how I knew that?"

Me: "Oooooh ... yes, I do see that ... WOW!"

Nancy: "You wanna hear something about your mother?"

Me: "Sure ... "

Nancy: (after thinking a bit) "She's gonna be a grandmother someday."

Me: "She is not only a grandmother, but she's also a great-grandmother!!"

Nancy: "SEE!!! (even prouder) I told you!"

Me: "I DO see! Soooooo ... if I have this right ... you predict things that have ALREADY happened?"

Nancy: "Exactly ... "

KARL

VISITED MOM TODAY. KARL called me over to talk with him. For some reason, he will only call me Mr. Scully. When he first arrived, he told me he used to live with his daughter. When the daughter's boyfriend moved in, he told Karl he was in the way. He and the daughter told Karl he had to find another place to live. Over the course of the last year, he has told me more about his situation. This was part of our conversation:

Karl: "My daughter and boyfriend asked me to come back to live with them."

Me: "Really? How do you feel about that?"

Karl: "I should be happy, right?"

Me: "I don't know ... should you?"

Karl: "Oh Mr. Scully, I'm not stupid. I know they have been living without my Social Security check for a year. They want me to think they miss me. The check is what they miss."

Me: "I am so sorry to hear that. It must hurt."

Karl: "It's tough, Mr. Scully. That isn't how she was raised. (looking around the large dining room, gesturing with his hands) But I look around and think … these people are my friends … and my family now … all of you. I have a life. I'm happy here. I may not see my daughter again, but I decided I'm not going back … a weight has been lifted."

I am amazed by his clarity. He's home.

MAUREEN

VISITED MOM TODAY. WHILE sitting at lunch, Maureen rolled up to us in her wheelchair. This was the conversation:

Maureen: "I'm sorry I haven't visited with you lately."

Me: "I didn't notice, but that's okay."

Maureen: "The lady at the desk doesn't want me to bother you when you're visiting your mom."

Me: "Really? You honestly aren't bothering me."

Maureen: "She thinks I'm gonna take advantage of you."

Me: "Take advantage of me? In what way?

Maureen: "Well ... you know ... sexually."

Me: "What?!? What did you say to her?"

Maureen: (rather indignant) "I told her ... I would NEVER do that!" (Then, in a hushed tone she continued.) "Although ... if I was younger, I would."

It's nice to know I've still got it!

CORRINE

VISITED MOM TODAY. WITH Christmas still on her mind, I had a conversation with resident Corrine over lunch. This is how it went:

Corrine: "Your wife came to visit yesterday."

Me: "Really! How's she doing?"

Corrine: "She's okay. But she was mean to your mother."

Me: "You're kidding ... in what way?"

Corrine: "She was yelling at her. I told her to get the hell outta here."

Me: "Wow ... thanks for standing up for Mom."

JOHN D. SCULLY

Corrine: "I told your wife I wouldn't tell you everything if she brought me a present today."

Me: "And what if she doesn't bring the present?"

Corrine: "I'm spilling my guts."

Geez ... my nonexistent wife sounds mean!

Angela

Visited Mom today. Spent some time with Angela, a resident in her 80s. This was our conversation:

Me: "How are you today?"

Angela: "I am exhausted."

Me: "Why are you so tired?"

Angela: "Did you know I am taking care of my mother in my home now?"

Me: "I didn't know that. How is she doing?"

Angela: "She's okay. She's very difficult. I do everything for her, and she hollers at me all the time. She doesn't appreciate anything I do."

Me: "Does your husband help?"

Angela: "Oh him … (sadly) He won't help with anything because I took my mother in."

Me: "I'm so sorry to hear this. What a difficult situation for you."

Angela: (smiling) "Someday I will have time to myself to do just what I want to do."

Heartbreaking that now is that time …

Gino

Visited Mom today. We sat in the recreation room with several residents gathered at round tables. Song sheets had been passed out and a karaoke-type video played on the large screen TV. An agitated resident, Gino, sat at our table. He'd get up, walk to the hallway, and come back. Then he'd get up again and walk to the window to look outside. He couldn't sit still. On his way back from the hallway, he tapped me on the shoulder. This was the conversation:

Gino: "When does the ship start moving?"

Me: "I'm not sure. We'll need to ask the captain."

Gino: "Do you know who he is?"

Me: "I do. I'll ask him when I see him."

Gino: "You don't mind doing that?"

Me: "I don't. But I'll do it later. I'm sure he's busy. Why don't you join us here for the sing-along?"

After delegating this task, he was able to relax and sing for the rest of the hour. He never mentioned the captain again.

GERT

VISITED MOM TODAY. WE sat at the end of the hallway after lunch. One of the residents, Gert, approached us and asked to speak to me in private. We went down the hallway just out of earshot of Mom. This was our conversation:

Gert: "You know, your mother and sister don't like your wife."

Me: "You're kidding ... why?"

Gert: "She's cheating on you."

Me: "Well ... that's a bummer. What should I do?"

Gert: "They want us to get together."

Me: "Oh really ... what do you think?"

Gert: (kind of annoyed) "Look ... I like you as a friend ... but my men gotta have hair."

BAM!

MARIA

VISITED MOM TODAY. WE sat with Maria, a resident who was born and raised in Portugal. She told me she talked her husband into coming to the United States before their two sons were school-aged. She knew there were better opportunities for all of them here. She and her husband worked in factories. She worked the overnight shift to be home days with their boys. They bought land and built a house, doing much of the work themselves. After sending their sons to college, they started going to Florida for vacations. She has six grandchildren, three from each son. The last one will finish college next year. She couldn't remember all their names or what they all did for jobs, but proudly knew there was an engineer, a teacher, and a scientist among them. This was how our conversation wrapped up:

Me: "It seems you made a good decision when you came to America."

Maria: (speaking in a thick Portuguese accent) "Oh yes ... I had a beautiful life! I am old now and here I sit (shrugging her shoulders) ... but it's okay. We could give our sons a beautiful life and now they give our grandchildren a beautiful life. I say, 'God Bless America' all the time ... every day ... (shaking a finger at me) and don't you forget to."

She had no idea it was July 4th.

KIMBERLY

VISITED MOM TODAY. WE were sitting at a table in the dining room. Kimberly, an 80-something resident, came to visit. She stood with her hands on Mom's shoulders. After some brief small talk, this was our conversation:

Kimberly: "I'm taking your mom to Florida to visit my sister."

Me: "Really! I hadn't heard. When are you doing that?"

Kimberly: "In a couple of days."

Me: "No kidding. How are you getting there?"

Kimberly: "We're driving."

Me: "Wow! That's exciting. It's a long drive."

Kimberly: "I know! Do you think you can give your mom money for gas?"

Me: "How much do you think gas will cost for the trip?"

Kimberly: (she sits now to talk business) "Well ... I think we'll need at least 50 bucks."

Me: "Not a problem. Let me know when your plans come together. I'll make sure she has spending money, too."

Kimberly: (smiling, pumping both arms in the air and looking at Mom) "We're gonna party! I'm calling my sister!"

Off she goes ... and I feel her excitement! It's real ... and contagious!

Not surprisingly, a half hour later she's talking about other things. No talk of Florida. No talk of money. No call to her sister.

Obviously, this road trip was never going to happen. But today ... for just a few minutes ... it sure felt possible.

Ellen

Visited Mom today. Due to Alzheimer's/dementia, our mom lost her ability to speak several years ago. Now, her smiles, eyes, and animated facial expressions say it all. Ellen, the resident we visited with today, greets me most days by saying that she's "going home today." Sometimes it's a big announcement, and other times it's a secret, told in hushed tones. Usually, the same conversation follows ... but not today. I brought Mom up in the conversation and it unexpectedly changed things. As she rolled her wheelchair toward me and motioned for me to lean forward to hear her whisper, I knew what was coming:

Ellen: "I'm going home today."

Me: "Oh no! I'm sorry to hear that. What will we do without you?"

Ellen: "Not sure — but it's time."

Me: "Well thanks for being so nice to Mom. I know she will miss you."

Ellen: "I'll miss your mother, too."

Me: "Really? What will you miss about Mom?"

Ellen: (she thought for a second) "I think I'll miss our talks."

Of all things … I felt tears burn my eyes … because that is what I also miss.

RENEE

Visited Mom today. On this beautiful summer evening, there was a concert outside on the patio. The air was warm and perfect for the occasion. The music was folk and very good. We sat next to Renee, a resident who likes to ask questions. This was our conversation:

Renee: (putting her hand on Mom's arm) "How old is she?"

Me: "She'll be 88 in October."

Renee: "Oh my. How long have you two been married?"

Me: (after regaining consciousness!) "I've known her for 61 years."

Renee: "How lucky you both are!"

JOHN D. SCULLY

She nailed that part ... we ARE lucky!

Alice

VISITED MOM TODAY. SHE was having a sleepy day, so we stayed in her room for lunch. About 45 minutes into my visit, another resident stepped in. She asked if she could sit in the room and read the history book she held up to show me. It was a thin picture book with historical stats. She'd been reading in the hallway but was distracted by all the noise. I said it was fine to stay and she settled into reading. At one point she asked if she could quiz me. Against my better judgment, I said yes.

Alice: "Where is the Liberty Bell?"

Me: "Philadelphia."

Alice: "Nope."

Me: "What???"

Alice: (kind of smug) "Pennsylvania."

Me: "Ohhhhh ... okay."

Alice: "Next question ... who was Alexander Hamilton?"

Me: "Oh ... that's the guy they wrote the Broadway musical about ..."

Alice: (looking at me bug-eyed) "Ummmm ... noooo! (reading from the book) He was the secretary of the treasury."

Me: "Oh, I know ... but they wrote a musical about his life ... uhhh ... never mind."

Alice: "Next question ... when was the 'decoration' of independence signed?"

Me: "1776."

Alice: "Yup ... finally! Next question ... what does the American flag represent?"

Me: "Freedom."

Alice: "Nope ... liberty ... for chrissake, did you sleep through school?"

Me: "Hey ... I was a good kid. Just not the brightest one."

Alice: (trying to make me feel better) "Now ... now ... now ... I'm not saying you're stupid ... you're just not very smart."

FRANK

Visited Mom today. It was another Sunday sing-along. We sat with Frank, a real gentleman. He was a former teacher and has such a kind way about him. In between songs, we would chat. This was one of those conversations.

Frank: "I became a grandfather again last week."

Me: "Wow! Congratulations! That is wonderful news."

Frank: "I've been a grandfather several times."

He paused for several seconds and then a bright smile came across his face.

Frank: "I don't quite remember the number of grandkids ... but I never forget the feeling!"

ROSE

VISITED MOM TODAY. WE sat together in her room since she was tired. After sitting quietly for a half hour, Rose, a very brash resident, spotted me and came in. This was our conversation.

Rose: "I've been looking for you."

Me: "What's up?"

Rose: "I'm trying to leave here."

Me: "And what do I have to do with that?"

Rose: "I wanted to know if I could move in with you."

Me: "Ummmm ... well, I only have one bedroom."

Rose: "That's ok. That's all I need."

Me: "But it's MY bedroom!"

Rose: "Oh ... well I can share it with your wife."

Me: (realizing the one-bedroom isn't dissuading her) "You know I live in Hartford, right? That's pretty far to visit your family and friends."

Rose: "Hmmmmm ... "

We sat in silence for a short time, then ...

Rose: "Well, I hate to do this to you, but I've gotta turn you down."

Me: "Oh darn it! That's too bad."

Rose: "I hope you're not mad."

Me: "Of course, I'm not mad. Still friends?"

Rose: "Still friends."

And off she went.

SANDY

VISITED MOM TODAY. MY mother's current roommate, Sandy, used to work in nursing homes. She often believes she is working now and taking care of Mom. Today we were sitting in the dining room after lunch. This was our conversation:

Sandy: (moves her chair close to me to talk quietly) "You know I love your mother, but I am thinking about quitting here. I can't take the petty stuff that goes on here."

Me: "Oh really? I'm so sorry to hear that. You know how much Mom likes having you around ... and how much we appreciate what you do for her."

Sandy: (she breaks out into a big smile and punches me in the arm) "Well ... aren't you a big pain in the butt ... making me feel guilty about leaving!"

We both have a good laugh — she blows Mom a kiss and goes "back to work."

VISITED MOM TODAY. I walked into the dining room where Sandy and Mom were sitting together. This was our conversation:

Sandy: "I took your mother shopping today." (Sandy was in her pajamas and slippers. Mom is confined to a wheelchair.)

Me: "Oh really? What did you shop for?"

Sandy: "Clothes. We bought the outfit she's wearing." (Mom is wearing a sweatsuit she's had for a couple of years.)

Me: "Nice! Seems like you both had a good time."

Sandy: (leaning over to talk quietly so mom wouldn't hear her) "I'm going to ask one of the other girls to get her ready for bed tonight. She kicked my butt shopping. I'm exhausted."

VISITED MOM TODAY. Mom's roommate, Sandy, has it in her head she is traveling somewhere. She's feeling the pressure of getting away and not leaving her "patient." As I visited with Mom, she walked into the dining room and sat down with us. This was our conversation:

Sandy: (rather stern) "Are you taking Mom home with you today?"

Me: "Ummmm ... I wasn't planning on it."

Sandy: (annoyed) "Well I'm going away, and I won't be here to take care of her."

Me: "I can't. I work all day."

Sandy: (really annoyed) "What's wrong with your wife? Can't she take care of her?"

Me: "Well she isn't specially trained the way you are."

Sandy: (smug and with a smirk) "Well ... that's true."

(an awkward silence — I hate having her mad.)

Me: "I'll tell you what, you know the staff here. Why don't you recommend someone you think would be best and I'll pay to have them take care of Mom while you're away."

Sandy: (thinks a moment) "That could work." (thinks some more) "I like that idea. I'm getting my clothes ready now. I'll give it some thought."

And she's off to pack ...

VISITED MOM TODAY. I was walking to her room to put clean laundry away when I saw (and heard!) her roommate, Sandy, kicking a male resident out of their room. The male resident quickly shuffled by, and then Sandy hurried over and grabbed my arm. She was red in the face and furious. This was our conversation:

Sandy: "That son of a gun was snooping around your mom's room!"

Me: "I'm sure he was just confused."

Sandy: "Well, I don't like it!"

Me: "I'm sure it won't happen again."

Sandy: "I'll kick his butt if it does!"

(She's so wound up ... I'm now slightly concerned about putting Mom's clothes in her closet and drawers ... so I tread lightly.)

Me: "You know I have Mom's laundry ... right?"

Sandy: (slightly puzzled) "Yeah."

Me: "You know I have to put it away in her closet and dresser, right?"

Sandy: (now annoyed) "Yeah ... so?"

Me: "So ... I want to make sure you don't think I'm snooping around ... and kick MY butt!"

Sandy: (she flashes a quick smile, then stink-eyes, shaking her fist in my face) "Don't get smart with me ... or I WILL kick your butt!"

She's probably 80 pounds soaking wet. But she scares me!

Betty, Donna, and Faith

VISITED MOM TODAY. WITH it dark early these days, I've noticed many residents sundowning. It is a symptom of Alzheimer's disease and other forms of dementia. It is also known as "late-day confusion" where confusion and agitation may get worse in the late afternoon. I didn't know what sundowning was until we experienced it with Mom. The staff had their hands full today with a couple of agitated residents. As I sat with Mom, helping her with her Dunkin' coffee and munchkins, Betty came to sit at our table ... anxious about where she needed to go. She ends her sentences by counting numbers. Donna moved to four different seats, with her walker, in the span of 10 minutes. She finally settled at our table in the chair next to me. Faith was sitting alone and intermittently

71

asking, no one in particular, what she was doing next. Since we were slowly gathering a posse, I brought Faith's wheelchair over to our table … wondering if it might help to be together. This was our conversation:

Me: "So now that we're all here, did everyone have a good day?"

Betty: "Where do we need to go? I don't know where I should be. 37, 38, 39."

Faith: "What are we doing now?"

Donna: (eyeing other chairs to move to)

Mom: (The heck with sundowning, she's got coffee and munchkins to eat! She's happy as can be!)

(Okay, my first question didn't click with anybody … I try another.)

Me: "Does everyone have a favorite Christmas Carol? Mine is Silent Night."

Betty: "Oh that's a good one. Do we need to go across the street? Where do we have to go? 43, 44, 45."

Faith: "What do we do next?"

Donna: (She tries to get up with her walker. I touch her arm and ask her to stay. She sits.)

(I try again …)

Me: "Does anyone have anything they'd like to talk about?"

(It's quiet for a minute.)

Donna: "I'd like to talk about my dress." (It's a purple and blue paisley housecoat.)

Me: "What would you like to say about your dress?"

Donna: "It's a happy dress."

Me: "And why did you wear a happy dress today?"

Donna: "Because I'm happy to be sitting with all these nice people."

For the next several minutes there were just smiles and nods around the table. We sat together, happy for quiet … and seemingly peaceful. An honest and healing moment.

LENA

VISITED MOM TODAY. WE sat with Lena, a 60-something resident who loves to tease me. She will give me a hard time with everything. She will consistently give the evil eye and pretend she's mad if I glance at my phone. She'll say, "Put that away ... and visit Mama." This was our conversation:

Me: "Our niece sent me pictures of her preschool class dressed up for Halloween. Look." (handing her my phone)

Lena: (after swiping through all the pictures) "I don't see a witch. I'd like to see a witch."

Me: "I think they did cute costumes, not scary ones."

Lena: (with a twinkle in her eye and a little smirk ... she started to tease) "Well it isn't Halloween without a scary witch. I'd like to see one this year."

Because of her sense of humor, I decided to turn the tables on her. I opened my camera app and switched the screen to the "selfie" position.

Me: "Oh here you go — you want to see a scary witch?"

I handed her the phone and there she was ... full screen! She screamed with laughter and fell back into her chair. We laughed that hard laugh ... mouth open, shoulders shaking, making no noise. When we stopped, she got up, shaking her head and smiling. As she handed me the phone with one hand, she punched my arm with the other hand and said:

"Put that away ... and visit Mama." (Evil eye and all!)

Diane

Visited Mom today. Because of the COVID-19 pandemic, the nursing home had been closed to visitors for 51 weeks. We were then allowed to visit, but everyone was still being cautious. We were wearing masks, keeping physically distant, and being asked to visit only with Mom and not gather with other residents. So, there wasn't an opportunity to engage in some of the conversations I have had in the past. Out of the blue, while sitting at lunch with mom, Diane, a resident I hadn't met before, rolled up in her wheelchair to say something. This was our conversation:

Diane: "I'm sure you're a nice guy and all, but I'm not interested in dating."

Me: "Okay. That's alright. Is there a problem?"

Diane: "Well ... how old are you?"

Me: "I just turned 64."

Diane: "Oh my God — too old."

She has to be at least mid-80s!

TERESA

VISITED MOM TODAY. WITH a small COVID outbreak, meals were served in rooms. While I sat with Mom for lunch, I had the opportunity to chat with her current roommate, Teresa. This was part of the conversation:

Teresa: "I had a good talk with your mom today." (Mom hasn't spoken in over eight years.)

Me: "Really! What did you talk about?"

Teresa: "The guy down the hall. I think he likes her."

Me: "That's interesting! What does she think?"

Teresa: "She doesn't like him that way."

Me: "Well ... then I guess he's available for you."

Teresa: "I'd only want him as a friend with benefits!"

Me: "What? You know what that means?"

Teresa: "Yeah ... a guy with money!"

And that's where we left it!

INEZ

VISITED MOM TODAY. FINALLY, pandemic restrictions were lifted and we were sitting in groups at meals again! Inez, who I would say is in her 90s, sat diagonally across from Mom. She had her hair cut. It was stylish, and it looked great! The residents have their hair done by a guy who stops in for a few hours each week. I leaned down by her chair to talk. This was our conversation:

Me: "Who did your hair? I love it!"

Inez: "Thank you. I was visiting my mother and her friend's son did it."

Me: "Wow! He's a good hairdresser. It is so stylish."

Inez: "Well, he's going to school to learn to cut hair."

Me: "Really! You are a brave person to let him practice on you. I'm sure that helps him."

Inez: (with a side-eyed glance and a smirk) "I only did it 'cause it was free."

June

Visited Mom today. We had a great conversation with June, a resident who was probably in her late 80s. Her career was in nursing. Not surprisingly, she thinks she is working at the nursing home. She usually greets me in her role as a nurse. She will give me her report on Mom or bring me to the nurse's station to check in or see me to the elevator so we can talk privately without Mom hearing. After lunch today, I was with Mom in a sitting area at the end of her hall. June came to check in with me. This was the start of our conversation:

June: (a hand on Mom's shoulder) "How does Mom seem to be doing?"

Me: "She seems a little sleepy today. How do you think she's doing?"

June: (Taking a seat on the couch next to me, she takes a deep breath.) "I've been meaning to catch up with you."

Me: "Is everything okay?"

June: "I'm not sure you know this ... but everyone on this floor has Alzheimer's."

Me: "Really. Well, thanks for letting me know."

June: "You know your mother lives on this floor, right?"

Me: "I do."

June: (pauses for a few seconds) "Do you understand what I'm trying to tell you?"

Me: "Ohhhhh ... you think Mom has Alzheimer's?"

June: "We do."

Me: "Well, I suspected something was going on."

June: "She's happy here and we take good care of her. Just make sure you keep visiting."

She went on to talk about her 13 and 16-year-old sons and her mother who lives with her and does all the cooking since she has to work all day. What a sweetheart! I wanted to take her home with me!

ROBERT

VISITED MOM TODAY. SHE is a slow eater, so we are usually the last ones to leave the dining room. As people were being taken back to their rooms, Robert, a male resident, got up and started clearing tables. As he made his way closer to us, this was our conversation:

Me: "It's nice you are helping out today."

Robert: "It gives me something to do."

Me: "I'm sure it's a big help to the staff."

Robert: "I like it and I'm happy to do it."

Me: (kidding) "Do you get paid?"

Robert: "Oh no. But they say thank you when I'm done. (stops and looks at me) You know, sometimes just saying thank you is the best pay you can get."

Karen and Julia

Visited Mom today. We had a great time watching as staff passed out beautiful, donated clothes to residents based on their size and/or personality. It was like Christmas! Julia was one resident at our table. She received a bright red blouse and was overjoyed with it. Karen, another resident at the table, was writing each person's name on the piece of clothing they were getting. This was a part of the conversation:

Karen to Julia: "Oh that red blouse is going to make you look hot."

Me to Karen: "I'm sure they'll find something hot for you, too."

Karen: (looking over her glasses): "My last and only hope for a hot body ... is cremation!"

LAURA

VISITED MOM TODAY. I was in the lobby waiting for the elevator. A woman resident, pushing her wheelchair backward
with her feet while sitting in it, was struggling to get over the
threshold to the elevator. Her name was Laura. I offered to help
her. This was our conversation:

Me: "Let me help you get over this hump." (as I grabbed the
wheelchair handles)

Laura: (not able to see me at this point) "You sound like a movie
star."

Me: "Well thank you ... I've never been told that before."

(I pulled her over the threshold, gently spun her around to face
the elevator, and stepped in front of her to introduce myself.)

Laura: "Oh my ... you're handsome, too. Although, my eyesight is very bad."

Hmmmmmm ...

Susan

Visited Mom today. We sat with a long-time resident who has always known me by my name. She is a sweetheart. Recently she began calling me "Father." When she called me "Father" today, I sat down to see if I could find out what she was seeing. I started with a generic question to see if I would get a clue. This was our conversation.

Me: "So ... when will we see each other again?"

Susan: "You'll see my dad and me at church on Sunday, Father."

Me: "Oh yes ... of course!"

Susan: "My dad loves your church."

Me: "That's so nice. And how about you? Do you like our church?"

Susan: "Yes. The only thing that worries me is when people come in late to Mass and then leave early."

Me: "Why do you think they do that?"

Susan: "I think maybe they are taking care of someone sick, or have a bunch of kids to get ready, or have to leave to go to work."

Me: "Do you think it's possible they are just trying to meet their Sunday obligation ... to be able to say they went to church without staying for the whole Mass?"

Susan: "I suppose that's possible, Father. But let's think better of them ... and pray that everything's okay in their lives."

My God ... we never know who our teachers will be.

Marcella

Visited Mom today. I've learned the best way to have a conversation with residents is to ask questions. The questions guide the conversation and keep them going. Today I spent time with Marcella, talking about a variety of things. I thought it was a good conversation. Here's how it wrapped up:

Marcella: "Don't you have to go?"

Me: "No. Not yet. (checking the time) I can stay a little longer."

Marcella: (a little sarcastically) "No ... are you sure you don't have to go?"

Me: "Oh ... do you want me to go?"

Marcella: "Well ... "

Me: "Am I keeping you from something?"

Marcella: "I'd like to go see my friends."

Me: "Oh that's fine. Not a problem. I hope I didn't hold you up."

Marcella: "No ... (as she rolled away in her wheelchair) But you sure ask a lot of damn questions!"

I need to "read the room" better.

Afterword

THIS VERY LAST CONVERSATION was specifically put at the end of this collection because of the resident's annoyance with me asking all the "damn questions." How ironic! It was always my questions that opened the door to each conversation. The answers gave me an idea of the person's reality at the moment. I would figure out where their mind was living and then ask questions that met them where they were. I would avoid questions that were unrelated to their reality or that would cause them to try to "remember" something. The questions were always the key to engaging people and keeping the conversations going.

I had wonderful conversations because I always kept the most important thing I learned in mind: step into their reality because they can no longer step into mine. I learned to be spontaneous and limber about what I asked in order to keep the conversations going. I liken it to being part of an improvisational troupe. Improv performers make up their dialogue as they go along, taking their cue from what was said last. It is the same concept when talking to a person living with Alzheimer's/dementia. They will also tend to be calmer, less frustrated, and less confused if they are allowed to live in their world, instead of being corrected, or unsuccessfully coaxed into ours.

Be open to whatever is being said. If you can determine where the person is in that moment; a different place, a different age, or a different time in their lives, then step into their reality, you will succeed at engaging your loved one. It took time, but I was able to find moments of lightness and beauty in the difficult journey of this disease. Our loved ones, living with Alzheimer's and dementia, deserve those moments, as do we.

Acknowledgments

I NEED TO ACKNOWLEDGE my husband, David Osella, for his unwavering support of this project. Your willingness to repeatedly read the manuscript and offer feedback has been invaluable. I am also grateful for your understanding and patience over the course of Mom's 15 years of living with Alzheimer's/dementia. You never complained once or made me feel guilty about arranging our plans around my multiple visits a week or being away from home for several hours at a time. You make even the hard things easier to manage.

To my siblings and their spouses, Bill and Stephanie Scully, Beth Scully and Eileen Barrett, Moira and John Myers, Jim and Kathy Scully, and Meg Scully, thank you for always sticking together through this journey with Mom. We could not have done this without each other's support. Mom and Dad gifted us with a strong sense of family, and I love seeing it alive and well in our next generation.

A huge debt of gratitude goes to my Facebook friends who embraced these stories the very first time I posted one. Although I dismissed your suggestions of publishing a book for a long time, you were persistent in your encouragement. It was your comments that planted the first seeds for this book, and your continual nudging that made this happen. Never underestimate the power of your comments!

My friend Mary B. Volk edited the first version of the manuscript, and I am so grateful for the care she took going through it. Her constructive criticism, her suggestions for changes, and her command of writing and punctuation gave me the confidence to send the manuscript to a publisher. I would not have done it without her stamp of approval.

Huge thanks to my creative nephew, Matthew Scully, for his willingness to team up with me on this project. When I heard I could have someone help design the book cover, I knew there was no other creative person I would want. His thoughtfulness and sensitivity as a person, in a world that does not always appreciate those qualities, make his work even more meaningful and amazing to me. I love that we kept it in the family!

My thanks also to Lisa Marshall, author of *Oh, Hello Alzheimer's* and advocate for caregivers, for spending time talking with me about how I might publish a book and providing me with contacts. This would not have happened without our conversations.

And to Elizabeth Hill, CEO and Publisher at Green Heart Living Press, thank you for taking a chance on a very new writer. Your support and encouragement gave me the confidence to see this through.

About the Author

In 2008, when their mother was diagnosed with "dementia of the Alzheimer's type," John and his five siblings began overseeing her care. Since 2011, they visited several times a week at a nursing home where she lived. Those visits were the impetus of this book.

A graduate of Curry College in Milton, Massachusetts, with a double major in communications and management, John worked for radio and television stations for the first eight years of his career. For 30 years after that, he worked for a media/advertising firm, the last seven of which, as President.

John retired in 2019 and is a volunteer end-of-life doula with Middlesex Health Hospice Program in Middletown, Connecticut. He and his husband David are active in their church,

JOHN D. SCULLY

Immanuel Congregational Church, United Church of Christ, Hartford, and live in West Hartford, Connecticut.

Instagram @visitedmomtoday

TikTok @visitedmomtoday

www.visitedmomtoday.com

Made in United States
North Haven, CT
22 October 2024

59313885R00061